Words of Praise for Games2Careers

"As the host of a Long Island job hunting and career planning television show, Jobline, which has survived the turmoil of television broadcasting for nineteen years, I have come to know Sue Gubing as a champion of career planning for adolescents and adults. As a member of the staffing and corporate outplacement community of Long Island for over twenty years, I have also watched Sue develop her ideas from passionate beliefs into a crystallized 'how to.' The concept of Games2Careers, *which, in unique fashion, uses a young person's natural abilities to stimulate career choices, is long overdue in print. I have no doubt this book will change the lives of countless students who are exposed to its wisdom. I believe that finding one's Career DNA will become one of the cornerstones of the entire career planning process in this millennium. Well done."*

—**Scott Passeser**, Director of Industrial Outreach for Stony Brook University, Host of News 12 Long Island's *Jobline*

"Everyone who knows Karen McKenna knows that she is amazingly passionate about helping people find their way in life. Karen is an unforgettable person whose enthusiasm and sense of possibility are matched by a wonderful ability to find practical resources and come up with solutions that are fun and on target. She simply has a great talent for helping people find direction. That's what makes reading this book so worthwhile. If you want to help your child, there isn't anyone better [than Karen]!"

—**David Rottman**, Founder and Former President of Career Counselor Consortium

"Child's play leading to career decisions is a novel approach for guiding students."

—**Cheryl Davidson**, Executive Director
of Long Island Works Coalition

"Sue Gubing brings the power we've always had within ourselves out in the open and forces us to explore new ways of looking at not only our own potential but that of our children's. It is a fascinating look at how we're hardwired to be what we want to be if only we look in the right places."

—**George Giokas**, President/CEO
of StaffWriters Plus, Inc.

GAMES 2 CAREERS

GAMES 2 CAREERS

CAREERS

Career Success is Child's Play

Gubing and McKenna

Legwork Team Publishing
New York

AuthorHouse™
1663 Liberty Drive, Suite 200
Bloomington, IN 47403
www.authorhouse.com
Phone: 1-800-839-8640

First published by AuthorHouse 3/6/2008

ISBN: 978-1-4343-7681-7

Legwork Team Publishing

Cover design, interior layout,
and print ready file by Legwork Team Publishing

Printed in the United States of America
Bloomington, Indiana

This book is printed on acid-free paper.

Footnotes:

1. Page 31, reference to multiple intelligences—*Frames of Mind: The theory of multiple intelligences*, New York: Basic Books. Gardner, Howard (1983; 1993) Second edition, Fontana Press, Britain
2. Page 32, reference to Dr. John L. Holland—*The Self-Directed Search and Related Holland Career Materials: A Practitioner's Guide*, Reardon, Robert C., PhD., Lenz, Janet G., PhD. PAR Psychological Assessment Resources, Inc., 1998, Odessa, FL., Page 31.
3. Page 121, reference to the Networking Event for Adults—based on "The Party" from *Your Ideal Job or Next Career*, Bolles, Richard N., Ten Speed Press, 1991, Berkley, CA, page 27.

We dedicate this book to parents, educators, and all who will use it to inspire children to reach their fullest career potential. May all who read this book find career fulfillment by recognizing and applying their natural interests and abilities.

Contents

Acknowledgments

Because many people have inspired the making of this book, there are too many names to include here. However, we would like to take this opportunity to sincerely express our deepest appreciation to all who have played a significant role in feeding our passion for career development. Without your constant support and guidance, Games2Careers may have never made it to the press.

We wish to thank Stephen Wirth, Jim Ryan, and Maggie Kalas for providing the setting for the final chapter in getting this book published. A chance meeting with Stephen led us to Jim, who shared his recent experience as an author. Jim introduced us to Maggie, and it all fell into place. Maggie has been our friend, mentor, sounding board, and connection to the publishing world. She helped us transform our raw material into a book that could appeal to and help many people. Our sincere appreciation goes to Janet and Yvonne at Legwork Team Publishing for their encouragement and enthusiasm. It is great to have access to a professional publishing team on Long Island.

And we would like to thank, in advance, all the parents and educators who will use the information in this book to make a difference in the lives of countless children.

—*Susan H. Gubing and Karen McKenna*

My deepest gratitude goes to my husband, Bill, and to my son, Bill, and his wife, Jessica, whose love, patience, wisdom, and undying support is a blessing to me every day.

Throughout my career, I have been fortunate to have many supportive people who allowed me to implement my creative ideas. Much thanks goes to all my supporters at the Smithtown Central School District, namely, career education advocates, Sherrion Elmore and Richard Collins, Dr. Christopher Gallagher, and Edward Ehmann, superintendent of schools. Their innovative leadership spurred me on to think in new and innovative ways.

Special thanks go to those family, friends, and colleagues—you know who you are—who would not let me forget about my promise to write a book. Thank you for not letting me shelve this project under any circumstances.

—Susan H. Gubing

More than anyone, I thank my husband, Rich, for *always* believing in me and inspiring me with his love and devotion. The last few years have been filled with change and adventure. As partners, we have flourished and grown closer. Without his understanding, flexibility, and support, this book would never have come to be.

Special thanks go to my mom and dad for encouraging me to follow my dreams. You've both always cheered me on in so many areas of my life. Without your love and guidance, I know I would have missed a great deal.

To my brother, Jim, and sister, Alison, I give my warmest appreciation for inspiring and believing in me. Knowing that you are there and always willing to help or just listen means the world to me.

Sincere gratitude goes to those colleagues who gave me my big break—the chance to work in career management. I thank

Mary Brown, Fran Kent, and Todd Morena for the opportunity to demonstrate my counseling skills at DBM.

I would also like to express my thanks to Kathy Rodgers and Kevin Waxman for remembering me when an opportunity arose with the Council for Adult and Experiential Learning (CAEL) to run a unique training grant program on-site at Chase Career Services. In particular, I want to thank David Rottman for creating an environment that let each of us shine. Under David's leadership, I felt free to bring my ideas to life while learning so much from the talented professionals working by my side.

Finally, there is a special place in my heart for Celia and Jillian, my "little sisters." You both amaze and inspire me. Spending time with you made me realize that I had a special talent for helping teens and young adults find their way in life. We will always be *family*.

—Karen McKenna

Preface

A Note From the Authors

My passion for career planning and workforce development stems from my early childhood fascination with the occupations of people who surrounded me. Reading books such as the Nancy Drew novels and biographies caught my interest because of people's roles in society. Even my Halloween costumes tended to be occupation related.

Although I can attest that my entrepreneurial parents played a big role in how I approached the world, it was more my inherent industrial curiosity that led me in the direction of my life's work. Setting up lemonade stands, selling newspapers door-to-door, and observing my mom and dad working diligently into the night hours all molded my future career path.

My educational route to earn my degrees to teach business education and career counseling was influenced by my natural interest in high school business courses and my varied work experiences for a New York City temporary employment agency, which allowed me to try out various careers during college breaks.

At the age of twenty-one, I found myself at the doorstep of the teaching career I would embrace for thirty-eight years at the

Smithtown Central School District in New York State. The door of opportunity opened for me to teach the foundations of business and to place students into entry-level positions. During these years, I found that I needed a system to help young people to make the appropriate career choices. The system was right in front of my eyes—*the games I played as a child led me to my career passion.* I knew this concept could lead my students to their ideal careers as well.

Eventually, a number of principles formed the foundation of my games to careers theory, which I now refer to as Career DNA (Dynamic Natural Abilities). Career DNA is comprised of several aspects of a person's career potential, namely their authentic interests, aptitudes, work preferences, personality traits, learning styles, multiple intelligences, and values.

Using this formula, I have assisted—and continue to assist— tens of thousands of students and professionals in making wise, timely career choices. Like baseball players stepping up to the plate with expert batting knowledge, my clients have their Career DNA and are ready to swing the bat for home run career choices.

Comprehending my own Career DNA has allowed me to transition from one playing field to another. My consulting firm, CareerSmarts, continually illuminates new entrepreneurial horizons—both for me and for my clients. As a career consultant, I am now able to share my expertise with many educators at the postsecondary level. Speaking at conferences, assisting schools in establishing career planning programs, providing individual counseling, and sharing the Games2Careers book with the world has certainly fulfilled my greatest career passion—helping others to realize their career goals. I suppose I will always be that enterprising girl who once sold lemonade from a stand—except now, I am selling career wisdom by the cupful!

—*Susan H. Gubing*

My *aha* moment came fifteen years into my career. In retrospect, I was lucky. Having hit an impasse where I was working, I opted to take a severance package that came bundled with outplacement counseling, which intrigued me. Taking advantage of every resource available, I threw myself wholeheartedly into the outplacement process. What I found surprised me. As I attended weekly meetings with other clients whose jobs had been down-sized, I discovered that I truly enjoyed helping them ramp up their career exploration and job search campaigns. Within a short time, I knew I wanted to explore a career for myself in outplacement and career counseling.

I took to it naturally and, with my years of experience as a corporate training specialist, it was a smooth transition. Working on a consulting basis, I had opportunities to work with individuals from varied backgrounds. I loved conducting workshops on topics like interviewing, networking, and maintaining a positive attitude during a job search.

Over the next few years, I successfully built my experience, expanded my professional network, and eventually landed a position at Chase Career Services. When you find your life's work, there is no denying it. You feel it every day—fulfilling and energizing. There's nothing quite like it. My passion was helping others to explore careers and to find the educational resources that would best prepare them for their chosen field.

Moving forward in my own career, I realized that most adults fell into their jobs or careers. It was rare for someone to have access to a professional career adviser. I couldn't help but think, "Why is that so?" It seemed to me that the only adults who received professional assistance with career planning and job search strategies were those who were laid off from their jobs somewhere along the line, maybe ten or twenty years into their careers. From my perspective, it seemed that our society placed little to no emphasis on starting the career planning process when we are young. Instead, we go off to college, or some other form of career training, and pick something at random to study. Then when graduation time comes, we use the college career center to land a job, not to examine our career aspirations.

I found that time and time again, adults who were let go by their employer and received outplacement services benefited greatly from access to expert career and educational advice. And as I got to know them as individuals, I realized that many adults were in unfulfilling careers anyway. Without professional guidance during secondary school, which should have been aimed at uncovering their true interests, values, and skills, many had just landed somewhere. Then the years went by and the financial responsibilities grew. Soon, even if the job or career turned out to be a disappointment, there was no easy way out. It would take time, money, and lots of energy to begin career exploration while working to pay the bills. The thought that kept surfacing in my mind was, "If students received career and educational advice in or before high school, they would have a much better chance of choosing a career that would make them happy and successful."

During those same years, I served as a mentor with Big Brothers Big Sisters of America. I had the pleasure of mentoring two young girls over a nine-year period. I thrived on being a role model for Celia and Jillian—helping them to see the world through the eyes of someone older. Although I didn't realize it at that time, my professional and volunteer roles began to converge.

Everything came together when I decided to launch my own business, CareerPoint Services, Inc. My mission was to help parents and their children to begin the career exploration process well before receiving college degrees, even before filling out college applications. I wanted to take all my hard-earned experience in the corporate world and use it to help young people to prepare themselves for their lives' work. If they spent time exploring their true interests, they could make better decisions about their careers and educational plans. Not only would they enter the working world with a much greater chance of success and fulfillment, they and their parents could save years and money by choosing their postsecondary education equipped with self-awareness and confidence.

Sue Gubing is well known and respected for her career as a school-to-work expert in the Smithtown Central School District. I met Sue several times over the years at professional associations and networking meetings. Once I started my business, I called Sue and asked if she could give me feedback on my business plans. During that first meeting at the Millennium Diner, Games2Careers was born.

Teaming up with Sue to write this book was another *aha* moment. My corporate background complemented her secondary education background and vice versa. It all came together. This book became a labor of love for us. Although I had never dreamed of writing a book, our thoughts and life experience flowed smoothly onto the pages.

I hope you will find Games2Careers helpful whether you are a parent of school-aged children, a teacher, a guidance counselor, a student, or an adult. In any case, the easy reading style of our story will certainly provide a platform of knowledge and inspiration that will ultimately lead to career success.

—*Karen McKenna*

Introduction

Solving the Career Success Puzzle

What role can parents play in helping their children to make good career decisions?

How can parents help their children to make sound decisions about education and careers?

Will children independently make the right career choices for success?

If children love to play sports, video games, dolls, or board games, could this lead to a career?

If children aren't interested in any one thing, how can parents help them with educational and career choices?

No one knows what they want to do in life until age twenty-five anyway, so why should parents worry about their children's future?

If you have found yourself pondering questions such as these, you are not alone. As parents, we naturally want the best for our children. The financial security and sense of fulfillment they will experience by choosing an appropriate career is a vital part of living a successful and happy life. But without the proper guidance, many students will make rush decisions about careers and college without career planning. That lack of planning can be costly. Parents and students can end up spending a great deal of money on a college education only for the students to flounder as they struggle to decide what they want to do or realize they don't like the career path they've chosen. The good news is that resources are available to both parents and students to ensure none of the above-mentioned scenarios ever happens to them.

Without planning, careers just happen.

Choosing a career is one of the most critical decisions we make in our lives. Our experience has taught us that most people seem to fall into a career with little or no planning involved. In fact, many adults never receive any professional career guidance until they are laid off from a job. At that point in their lives, they are typically somewhere in the middle of their working years and were not expecting to be back out looking for work. The lucky ones will receive a severance package and some outplacement (career) counseling.

Through that counseling, many people realize that they don't truly enjoy the career they chose. With the help of a career counselor, they embark on new personal adventures to explore all the possibilities and learn a great deal about themselves along the way. Armed with this vital information, many are able to change to new careers with a higher probability that they will actually like the choices they have made.

Why not introduce this type of counseling and support at an earlier age? If more students in the K–12 system could learn career planning as an integral part of their education, they would stand a much better chance of understanding the world of careers and choosing one based on what they love to do.

Can the games we played as children provide clues to future career success?

Absolutely! We created this book primarily to help parents learn how to guide their children toward careers through their true interests. Our inspiration is quite simple. When children play, they choose to do the things they are naturally drawn to the most. Therefore, the games and toys that they choose represent their purest and most basic desires. Bridging a child's authentic interests with specific educational preferences and career objectives is the first of several layers in determining a person's Career DNA (Dynamic Natural Abilities). We've taken this one particular concept and developed a storyline format to illuminate the many clues available to parents as their children are growing up. Our story features an average family that presents various scenarios into the career planning process. You see through their experiences just how much parents can learn by observing their children and encouraging them to follow their dreams throughout their lives. It also highlights how adults can revisit their childhood interests to uncover links to making appropriate career decisions or changes.

Games2Careers is a different kind of career planning guide. It is designed to turn what could be a tedious task into an enjoyable and enlightening experience. Our objective in using our fictional family's story was to create a comfortable, entertaining format for absorbing career planning information. Rather than turning parents into career counselors, it is our goal to show parents how they can learn a great deal about their children's potential by simply observing them at play. Once parents share these observations with their children and their school counselors, students can more easily create winning educational strategies and ultimately enjoy successful careers. And, parents, you will have peace of mind in knowing that your children have the right pieces to solve their career success puzzle!

We are confident that Games2Careers will solve a few mysteries for anyone in the career planning process, and we encourage you share it with friends and family. But most importantly, we hope that the premise of our book reveals that career planning can be fun!

PART I

Choosing a Career
is Child's Play

1

Meet Paul and Amanda Holmes and Their Family

"We are so proud of each of you! And we are thrilled that you have all found careers that not only allow you to make a living but also allow you to do the work you love. Cheers!" Paul Holmes declared, as he raised his glass in a toast to his family.

It was a warm June night, and the Holmes family had gathered to celebrate career successes. This was a truly special occasion for the entire family, given the experiences they had and the lessons they learned over the previous several years. To fully appreciate their experiences, let's go back and find out exactly what led up to this celebration.

Their introduction to career planning was as memorable as it was sudden. Paul Holmes came home from his office one night with some surprising news. His job as a computer programmer for a prestigious and successful software company was being outsourced to a foreign country. At that time, many companies were sending technical jobs overseas, where they would only have to pay a fraction of Paul's salary for someone to do the same programming functions.

That night, as Paul sat at the kitchen table with his wife, Amanda, a look of disbelief came over his face. He reminisced about the twenty years he had spent working for that firm, how much he had enjoyed his job, and about the friendships he had developed with his colleagues. It seemed impossible. How could it all be gone? What was he going to do? He had a wife and four children to support. He and Amanda had been through a lot over the years, and they always got through the tough times together. This, however, was not something he was at all prepared for at this point in his life.

Paul had recently turned forty-one, and Amanda was forty. Their children were close in age too; with Bill the oldest at sixteen, then Ed at eleven, and the twins, Sarah and Chad, the youngest at eight. Paul's head was spinning as he thought about the situation and what a difficult time this was for him to lose his job. His manager had given him the name of an outplacement counseling firm he could consult with while looking for a new job. But right at that moment, his mind was focusing on his wife and children.

Paul and Amanda had been in their twenties when they married. Paul had settled into his job as a junior programmer, and Amanda had been working as an art teacher in an elementary school after graduating from college with a degree in fine arts. When Amanda was pregnant with Bill, they made a joint decision that she would stay at home to raise him and the other children they hoped to have. It was all looking pretty good for them.

Over the next eight years, they had Ed and the twins. Amanda was content and loved that she could be home with the children while they were growing up. Back then, no one had imagined that good paying jobs in the United States would soon be sent overseas in the increasingly competitive global marketplace.

2

Paul Learns About His Career DNA

"I'm a bit nervous about going to this outplacement office for the first time," Paul said as he got ready to leave the house. Amanda leaned over, touched his hand, and said, "I can definitely understand why you feel that way. After all, it's a new experience, but I have a good feeling about it. I think you'll find it helpful in deciding what to do next."

About two weeks had passed since Paul had received word that his job was moving offshore. So Paul had called the outplacement firm and made an appointment to talk to his career counselor, Maggie. His first meeting with Maggie was encouraging. She spent time talking to Paul about a concept known as Career DNA. She explained that every person has specific threads or characteristics that can guide them toward making successful educational and career decisions. This Career DNA consisted of authentic interests, aptitudes, work preferences, personality traits, learning styles, multiple intelligences[1], and values. To help uncover Paul's Career DNA, Maggie decided to begin by focusing on his interests as a child.

Exploring Childhood Interests

Maggie asked Paul to think back to his childhood years and identify the games and toys he loved to play. Paul was taken aback by this question. "How can my childhood games have any relationship to my future career choice?" She went on to explain that as children, we have no worries, no outside pressures, no responsibilities to meet. We are in the most relaxed stage of our lives. We, therefore, choose games and toys we wish to play that match our true interests. By exploring the games we played as children, we open insights to our genuine passions and work preferences.

This concept intrigued Paul. He thought back to his life between ages four through ten. He remembered that reading, completing crossword puzzles, visiting museums, and collecting rocks and stamps always interested him. In fact, his most treasured childhood toy was his stamp album. He also liked to organize his collections. Paul loved playing card games and counting his money. In his teenage years, Paul grew to like analyzing the stock market and, with the help of one of his favorite uncles, he had a chance to invest a few dollars. Maggie suggested they set up another appointment later that week to continue their discussion and look deeper into Paul's true interests.

Childhood Interests Reveal Career Potentials

At the next appointment, Maggie told Paul about an assessment from the extensive work of Dr. John L. Holland[2], a retired professor from Johns Hopkins University, who developed the RIASEC Theory, or Holland Code. His theory states that all people fit into one or more interest groups or personality traits: Realistic, Investigative, Artistic, Social, Enterprising, or Conventional.

Maggie explained to Paul that an analysis of his interest groups was the first link to understanding his Career DNA. This assessment would help him make sense of his unique career potential. Paul was excited to learn more and to complete the assessment right away.

Paul Determines His Interest Code

Paul's assessment began with him imagining that he was at an event where several groups of people were gathered to network. Each group was discussing specific topics. Paul needed to decide the top three groups he would be most comfortable joining.

Here are the six interest groups:

Realistic
People who have athletic or mechanical ability, prefer to work with objects, machines, tools, plants, or animals, and/or like to be outdoors.

Investigative
People who like to observe, learn, investigate, analyze, evaluate, or solve problems.

Artistic
People who have innovating or intuition abilities, like to work in unstructured situations, and use their imagination and creativity.

Social
People who like to work with people to enlighten, inform, help, train, or cure them, or are skilled with words.

Enterprising
People who like to work with people to influence, persuade, perform, lead, or manage for organizational goals or economic gain.

Conventional

People who like to work with data, have clerical or numerical ability, carry out tasks in detail, or follow through on others' instructions.

Paul made his first, second, and third choices. The first three letters of each group created his interest code, which was ICE—Investigative, Conventional, and Enterprising. The investigative aspect made sense to Paul because his work in software development had always involved analyzing data, observing systems and solving problems. Paul found that the conventional category fit him well too. He couldn't believe it. This was all so true.

The final letter E, for enterprising, surprised Paul; he never really saw himself as influential and persuasive. Maggie explained that the first letter in the code shows the most dominant interest that a person may have; the second and third letters in the code are the next most prevalent interests. Although E was not his first or second code, Maggie emphasized that it was still important information for Paul to consider as he began to think about what he wanted to do *next*.

Maggie asked Paul to think back to last week's meeting at which he identified his childhood games. He realized that his preferences for activities such as reading, completing crossword puzzles, visiting museums, and collecting stamps and rocks, clearly indicated his investigative nature. Furthermore, his desire to organize, play card games, and count money highlighted his conventional tendencies. As it turned out, Paul's love for following the stock market reflected his enterprising spirit.

Paul wondered how all this related to choosing a new career. Maggie explained that even though the three interest codes are listed in order based on how strongly they suit an individual, any combination of those letters could be considered when identifying potential careers. That meant Paul could use any of the following combinations when envisioning careers he might like to pursue: ICE, IEC, CIE, CEI, ECI, EIC. Therefore, using all six interest code combinations provides more insight and additional choices worth considering.

Curiously, Paul asked Maggie about her interest code and how it related to her chosen profession as a career counselor. She told him her code was SAE. As a child she liked to play teacher and volunteered at the local YMCA to student coach basketball. Her love of helping people often spilled over at church as an advocate for teens. When evaluated, she wasn't surprised to find that social was her dominant interest group. The next group, artistic, was also easy since Maggie's natural creativity showed up in all of her interests: fictional writing, learning several languages, and the theatre arts. She confessed to Paul that the last was a challenge since she not only tended to take charge in group settings (enterprising), but she also enjoyed being outdoors and physically active (realistic). In the end, enterprising better suited her social nature, along her with strong leadership skills. Now, as a senior counselor at the agency, she not only manages the department, she works directly with a variety of clients—from academic and athletic students to business professionals to Spanish speaking immigrants—all seeking innovative ways to achieve career success.

By the time Paul got home that evening, impressed by all he learned, his mind was racing. He couldn't wait to share the assessment results with Amanda and talk about what they meant for him, and for their family's future. Things were starting to look brighter. Maybe there was more out there than working as a programmer for a giant company. The possibilities started to swirl in his head. He had trouble sleeping that night. He was thinking about what all this meant and which careers might be a good match for his skills and interests. In a way, he felt strange—although he had lost his job, he was no longer dwelling on his past; instead, he found that he was excited about the future. What Paul could not know, was the impact his experience with the outplacement firm, his counselor, and his Career DNA results would have on his entire family.

3

Amanda Ponders Her Career Choices

"Well, I guess it's time for me to think about what I would like to do as well," Amanda said after hearing how excited Paul was about his meetings with his career counselor. Paul smiled and said, "I think that's a great idea. We can explore new career directions together and share our experiences as we go along."

After dinner one night, Amanda and Paul sat down to discuss her interests. In college Amanda majored in fine arts. She always dreamed about owning her own art gallery or teaching art to young children. She remembered as a child how she was always drawn to the arts and crafts section of a store. Rather than buying a pre-made product in a box, Amanda always preferred to make her own crafts. She would continually create what she called masterpieces and give them away to her uncles, aunts, and grandparents for display on the refrigerator. Many times her creative efforts were rewarded with a dollar for her piggy bank. Uncle Robert told her repeatedly, "One day, Amanda, you are going to be a great artist!" Her artistic talents even extended to designing unique outfits for her dolls. As she got older, she found herself dressing in nonconforming styles. She liked the latest looks and was not afraid to try something new.

Amanda never had a chance to pursue a career in the art world because she and Paul married just six months after she finished college. Within their first year of marriage, she became pregnant with their first child. For a brief time, before she married Paul, Amanda found great satisfaction in teaching art to young children. She was lucky enough to get a leave replacement position at a local elementary school. Now she wondered what she should do. Could she find a rewarding career after years of raising a family? Paul shared the Holland Interest Inventory with Amanda. She discovered that her interest code was ASE—Artistic, Social, and Enterprising.

Amanda found the whole concept intriguing! She decided to use these new insights to do some research and explore potential career paths that matched ASE. As she thought back to her childhood, she could see how her favorite activities related directly to ASE. She clearly had a love for art—designing dolls' clothes, painting masterpieces for her family to display, and creating her own games. She had also displayed her strong social interest while teaching art. Now it all made sense. All those years that she dreamed of owning her own art gallery came from a lifelong interest in art within a social setting, running her own enterprise. She found it reassuring to know that her dream career was a true reflection of her most basic interests.

Since she already had a bachelor's degree in fine arts, Amanda wasn't sure if returning to school was important, or even necessary, but she did not want to rule it out. She decided to learn as much as possible about the potential careers that matched her interests. The assessment results made selecting potential careers easy with a list of all the careers that corresponded to her ASE code. If she wanted to consider even more possibilities, she could look at the potential careers associated with each combination: AES, SEA, EAS, ESA, and SAE.

She thought, "Wouldn't it be great if everyone had an opportunity to do the assessment before considering a career?" Every individual would have a menu of career choices matched by personal interests. Amanda decided to find out as much as possible about some of the additional career paths indicated by her assessment. At first, it was not easy to choose just a few possible careers for consideration, but she took her time and finally settled on:

1. teaching art at the elementary school level
2. running an art gallery
3. running an art supply store

By limiting herself to a few appealing options, she could devote more time to researching each one. Since she was only conducting research, even if none of these careers turned out to be what she would like to pursue, she could easily go back to the assessment report and pick three more to consider. In fact, she could repeat that process until she found the best choice for her.

Amanda jumped at the chance to learn more about the three careers she had chosen. From what Paul had learned from Maggie, his counselor, Amanda decided to visit a few galleries and art supply stores and have informational interviews with the owners. It is an effective method to learn as much as possible about a career before spending time and money on an education or on a business. You simply interview a few experts, asking them questions about what they do. It is an easy endeavor since most people are flattered to be asked for their opinions about their work.

The first week, Amanda visited three galleries in the closest city. She had set up appointments by checking with a few friends who knew someone at a gallery. Because someone with a direct connection to each gallery had referred Amanda, it was easier for her to get appointments than if she had cold-called. This turned out to be an extremely helpful exercise for Amanda. Although there were things she found she liked about running a gallery, overall, she decided that the long hours (evenings, special events, cocktail parties, and public relations activities) would be too much for her. She still had young children to raise.

It was time to check into another potential career choice. She decided to stop by a couple of art supply stores in the area and speak to the owners about the day-to-day activities she could expect in that business. The more she heard about the business, the more she liked it. Amanda felt strongly that she would enjoy meeting the people who came into the store each day—art teachers, children doing special art projects, and professional artists. She immediately felt that the environment and interactions she would have at an art supply store would be more to her liking than those at a gallery.

She had a strong inclination to move forward with an art supply business. Paul suggested that she still investigate teaching art before making any final decisions. Although she had worked briefly as an art teacher after college, twenty years had passed and the environment might have changed.

Over the next two weeks Amanda scheduled breakfast meetings with friends who had been teaching art for years. She liked the schedule, which would give her more time with her own children. As much as she enjoyed teaching, she still felt the need to be her own boss. Of the three careers she had chosen to explore, owning an art supply store was the only one that met her deepest desires as an artistic, social, and enterprising person. Things were starting to fall into place. When she shared her findings with Paul that evening, they laughed because all these new and exciting possibilities came to their attention because Paul had lost his job! Suddenly the future seemed full of opportunities for both of them.

Since Paul was going through his own career transition, Amanda felt that this was not the appropriate time for her to start a new business. Instead, she got a part-time job at a local art supply shop. This gave her a chance to try out the environment before making any financial commitments. Working part-time hours from ten a.m. through two p.m. each day balanced well with her responsibilities at home. She decided to continue working part time until she felt comfortable moving forward with her business plans.

Paul and Amanda found the whole experience interesting. They had learned a great deal about themselves and could see how the games they played as children had been key indicators of their strongest interests. They thought, "We're in our forties now, and this has opened up so many possibilities for us. Imagine what this exercise would do for the children!" By focusing on the toys, games, and activities that each of their children loved, Paul and Amanda could now guide them to investigate potential careers to match what they love to do. Paul said, "Who knew that choosing a career was child's play?"

PART II

Everyday Clues for
the Holmes Family

4

Bill the Persuader

"Dad, take a look at this model I just finished building," Bill called out from the family room. "It came out awesome," he added, "and I'm going to add it to my collection."

Bill was all boy. He had a room packed with Lego bricks, G. I. Joe action figures, model racecars, and ice hockey goalie equipment. Bill would not sit still to draw a picture. A crayon or paintbrush never touched his hand. However, if you gave him a hammer, screwdriver, or some type of tool, he could figure out why something was not working and fix it. His grandmother always told him that he was just like his grandpa, who she playfully referred to as "a man who could solve all world problems with a diagram and a toolbox." Like his grandfather, Bill had strong analytical skills and a desire to make money. He was always thinking about the final outcome and how he could persuade others to complete a project. At fifteen, he started his own lawn mowing business. He persuaded ten local homeowners to accept his offer to provide weekly lawn service for the entire summer. He was good at managing time, money, and customer requests.

When Bill entered eleventh grade at the local high school, Paul and Amanda knew it was time for him to make some decisions about his postsecondary education. They met with Bill's counselor to discuss his interests, his final two years of high school, and his choices for college majors. Because of Bill's childhood preferences and interest code results of ERI—Enterprising, Realistic and Investigative, the counselor suggested that Bill focus on two career options: engineering and business. The counselor suggested that Bill continue with all the required academic courses for high school graduation and college admissions while adding technology and business courses to his schedule. Under the counselor's advice, Bill added engineering, aeronautics, metal shop, automotive repair, accounting, marketing, business law, and keyboarding to his final two years of school. The Engineering teacher encouraged Bill to join the Robotics Club, in which Bill learned a good deal about mechanical engineering. He also joined the school's business club, DECA, as it fortified his interest in business operations. The school's work-based learning coordinator assisted Bill in finding employment at a local engineering firm. This experience gave Bill real-world insight into the daily tasks an engineer handles.

During the summer before Bill's senior year in high school, he and his parents visited a variety of colleges that had both engineering and business majors, not to mention ice hockey teams he could join! Paul and Amanda did a good job preparing Bill for his college major decision. The combination of Bill's high school courses, club activities, and work experience allowed Bill to focus on two college major options.

5

Ed the Doer

"Bill, when you get a chance, would you look at my ten-speed bike?" pleaded Ed. "There is something wrong with the timing. I know you can fix it. On Saturday morning, I want to join my friends at the park. We are going to race through the bike paths, and I want to win."

E d was very personable, liked by other students and pretty much everyone he met. He loved to play outdoors and to participate in sports of all kinds. He had been an extremely active child since an early age. If he wasn't kicking or hitting a ball, he was helping others with their skills. As a child, Ed had also liked to play cops and robbers or pretend he was driving a car. Paul and Amanda were proud of Ed's athletic accomplishments, as he was constantly chosen for school teams and played an important role on each one. He was often selected as team captain because of his sincere, non-assuming personality. Paul and Amanda felt they should observe Ed's preferences for games, toys, and activities and use that information to help guide him toward career options that would make him happy.

Ed's behavior extended to his friends in many ways. His friends sought him out if they wanted to share a problem or look for an answer. Ed took great interest in family and friends if they were sick or injured. He was both a nurturer and a good listener. If any of the children got into an argument, Ed was the one who served as the referee to make both sides feel pleased with the outcome.

The school system that the Holmes children attended had recently adopted the policy of creating career plans for all children, grades K–12. Ed's middle school counselor explained that the career plan would act as a road map for Ed's career options after high school. The career plan included information about the child's interests, personality, aptitudes, skills, courses, clubs, teams, work-based learning experiences such as shadowing, interning, and work experience, and future career options.

The middle school counselor determined Ed's interest code was RSC—Realistic, Social, and Conventional. In planning Ed's high school years, she suggested that he focus on health sciences, technology, and business courses. She advised Ed to continue with his interest in athletics, but added that he should also explore coaching at a summer camp and volunteering at a hospital. Both of these activities would allow Ed to learn more about the recreation and healthcare fields. She suggested that Ed seek out high school shadowing experiences with a sports trainer, a physical education instructor, and a police officer, and together they added these suggestions to Ed's career plan. He would have a chance to reflect on these activities by writing about his opinions, preferences, and discoveries in the career plan. His family and the counselor would review the plan each year.

6

The Twins: Sarah the Thinker and Chad the Organizer

"It's pretty amazing that they are actually twins," Amanda said with a laugh. "You would never know it by looking at which toys and games they each chose."

Sarah was an inquisitive child and loved to learn. She enjoyed solving puzzles, reading, playing board games, and loved her telescope more than anything. Sarah spent hours online exploring topics like astronomy and archaeology. For Sarah, it was important to get her library card once she was old enough. She enjoyed going to the library where she could spend hours sitting in the corner of the children's encyclopedia section. Her teacher had recommended she spend some time reading a series of books called *The Way Things Work,* which Sarah found fascinating. When she was home, she was either working on an experiment like creating a real volcano from a kit, or watching exploration and discovery programs on TV. Since Sarah loved astronomy the most, she had stars and constellations on the ceiling in her room.

Sarah signed up to be a Junior Girl Scout and quickly earned a number of badges, including Aerospace, Earth Connections, and Sky Search. Because of Sarah's strong interest in science, Paul and Amanda often took Sarah to science museums and planetariums. Sarah could literally spend all day wandering around the museum, trying to take it all in and learning as much as she could. The planetarium shows were also amazing.

When planning family vacations, Paul and Amanda tried to pick places where each of the children could have fun and get to do activities they really enjoyed. Although it could be challenging, given their different interests, the family always went on great vacations. Before returning home from each vacation, the children were already planning their next trip!

The most memorable vacation for Sarah was the family's trip to Washington, DC. She had dreamed of visiting the Smithsonian Institution and was particularly eager to see the Air and Space Museum. One part of that trip stayed with her for a long time—going to the IMAX theater to see the film *To Fly*. Sarah couldn't wait until she would be old enough to fly herself.

In school, whenever her science teacher needed help with a project, Sarah jumped up to volunteer. It gave her a chance to help other students understand and appreciate some of the scientific subjects that she took to so naturally. When her school introduced a new club about science and technology, Sarah signed up right away. She couldn't wait to go home that night and tell her parents all about the club and some of the planned activities and events. During parent-teacher conferences, Sarah's science teacher encouraged Amanda and Paul to find a science summer camp for her to attend.

When it came time to prepare Sarah's required career plan, with her teacher's help, Sarah found out that her interest code was

IRS—Investigative, Realistic, and Social. Her teacher encouraged Sarah to continue to participate in the science club and science courses such as astronomy and physics.

Even though Chad was Sarah's twin, his interests were entirely different. He collected baseball cards, stamps, and coins. He would often play office with a toy telephone, a desk, and some office supplies. He was great at organizing. From a young age, he even loved to organize the house! Amanda was thrilled with him— with four children in the house, she knew she could always count on a cheery Chad to help her to get the house in order. He also helped his dad with his business. The more time he spent setting up, organizing, or straightening up everything around him, the happier he was.

In order to help get his career plan organized, Chad spent some time with his teacher talking about his favorite activities. Chad immediately mentioned his beloved collections! He was an avid collector of baseball cards and coins since he was five. Each evening, he'd anxiously wait for his dad to come home so he could look through the coins his dad had in his pockets for any he needed to complete his collection books.

Chad's interest code was CIE—Conventional, Investigative, and Enterprising. His teacher recommended that he concentrate on business courses and suggested he join the student government. She also thought Chad would enjoy visiting local government offices to find out first hand what day-to-day activities took place there.

As it turned out, he loved the trip to Washington, DC, as much as Sarah. The Smithsonian was a great place to take all the children. With diverse exhibits and museums, there was literally something for everyone. Chad loved viewing the rare coins and gems. He couldn't believe how many collections were on display. He was just as happy to tag along with Sarah to see the Space and Science Museum. Remember, although Chad was primarily conventional, he was also investigative. He and Sarah were both interested in museums with interactive exhibits so they could learn how things worked. While they were still in Washington, DC, they made a trip to the United States Mint. This turned out to be the highlight of the trip for Chad. For a child who spent so much time collecting coins, it doesn't get much better than the Mint!

1

Signs Beyond the Playground

One evening Amanda was standing in the living room with her hands on her hips, just looking around, when Paul came up beside her and said, "What are you thinking about?" Amanda replied, "I was thinking about redecorating the living room. I'd like to add more color, maybe even buy some new furniture." "Amanda, you always have an idea for some interesting new project." "Well, I may come up with the ideas, but you're the one who makes them a reality!"

Paul and Amanda were discovering that their natural preferences reflected both the careers they chose and the daily tasks in their lives. Being artistic, Amanda always found ways to create a warm, homey environment for the family. As a thinker, Paul was always quick to jump in and tackle minute details to solve problems. They could also see how their children demonstrated their unique basic styles. Bill, the persuader, would motivate everyone about a potential weekend destination. Ed, the doer, would pack the car. Chad, the organizer, would map out the entire trip in great detail, and Sarah, the thinker, would investigate all the places they could stop along the way. They even noticed how each of their favorite TV channels and particular shows reflected their individual styles.

Television Programming Preferences

Holmes Family	Interest/ Descriptive	Television Preferences
Paul and Sarah	Investigative/ Thinker	History, discovery, science, detective, environment, animal behavior and habitat
Amanda	Artistic/Creator	Home design and decorating, arts dramas, musicals, animation
Bill	Enterprising/ Persuader	News, infomercials, finance, leadership, management, politics
Chad	Conventional/ Organizer	Game shows, sports scores and weather statistics, antiques and collectibles
Ed	Realistic/Doer	Adventure, sports, do-it-yourself, food/ cooking, or little or no television
	Social/Helper	Situation comedies, dramas, soap operas, romance, talk shows

Playing Computer or Video Games

Paul and Amanda found that each member of their family had unique preferences when it came to the home computer and to video games. Technology today has greatly changed the way people express their personality traits. How one uses the computer or other electronics is greatly influenced by their natural choices. If we take a look again at the six interest groups and match them up with the Holmes family's computer and video activities, we find that they also correlate with each member's dominant or secondary code.

Interests Matched with Holmes Family Video Game and Computer Activity

Realistic

Ed preferred video games with action, such as car racing, search and destroy games, and war reenactments. He enjoyed downloading new software and handling the hardware in connecting wires and wireless connections.

Investigative

Sarah and her father, Paul, chose games that called for analysis of clues, strategy, and problem solving. They used the computer to search for data in order to solve problems.

Artistic

Amanda preferred games which called for drawing, design, layout, and adding colors. She used the computer in creating artwork, working with digital photos, and creating Web pages.

Social

Ed also liked activities that included communicating with friends via e-mail or instant messaging. He frequented Web sites which related to networking and entertainment sites.

Enterprising

Bill's game preference was anything that included money, buying, selling, and other business ownership activities. He often used the computer to validate data such

Conventional	as stock market prices or to find the best price for a purchase.
Conventional	Chad played games with data recall, such as Jeopardy!® and Millionaire. He stayed organized on the computer by keeping an up-to-date calendar with his daily activities and events, he used virtual maps in traveling, and liked to record lists of personal possessions such as baseball cards and other collectibles.

Now let's see how these computer-related activities directly connect to appropriate career choices. If any of the Holmes family decided upon a career solely by how they used the computer for more than three hours a day, you may find them in the following career- or work-related situations:

- Ed as a computer network technician or hardware engineer. Because Ed's social inclination is nearly equal to his realistic interests, he could also find himself using the computer to teach online or to communicate with his students' parents.
- Sarah and Paul as engineers, chemists, anthropologists, economists, or pharmacists.
- Amanda as a Web site designer or an interior designer.
- Bill working in the field of finance, management, or operations management.
- Chad working in accounting, information technology, or office administration.

Play Preferences: Together or Alone

Amanda noticed other clues to the children's styles. She found that by observing their preferences for how they played games with others, she could see the connections to their interests and the choice of careers they would enjoy—a preference for playing alone or with others could have a strong connection to career choices.

One observation was that Sarah enjoyed playing alone for hours at a time. She could immerse herself in a science-fiction world and be extremely happy. On the other hand, Bill could not bear to be alone and needed to be around other people while he played. Amanda realized that if another person was not available, then Bill needed to blast the television or radio while doing his homework. Sarah enjoyed endless hours researching in a quiet laboratory setting while Bill flourished in a chaotic, people-filled environment.

In addition to matching career choices to games and interests, each individual needs to examine career choices that are influenced by interactions with people and environmental setting. Many individuals enjoy a blend of working alone and with others. However, then the question is, which environment is preferable for each person?

Team Play: Offense or Defense

Paul picked up on another interesting concept: How children choose which positions they play on a team relates to their personalities and, ultimately, to their career choices. In many popular sports, team positions are either offense or defense. For example, Bill, a goalie in soccer and ice hockey and a catcher in baseball, clearly preferred to play defense. Bill was protecting the team from losing.

On the other hand, Ed preferred positions such as a forward, pitcher, and quarterback, which are all offense. Driven to win the game for the team, Ed wanted to score when he played sports.

In the work world, Bill would flourish when the action of the day comes to him; Ed would want to go to the action. Bill would make a great engineering project manager while Ed would be a dynamic sales director or police officer.

Career DNA
Internal Factors That Influence Our Career Decisions

Career DNA is comprised of several key elements that are derived from an individual's intrinsic desire rather than an external influence. Within each strand of DNA, or dynamic natural abilities, a person can reveal key insights about their potential. Ultimately, a Career DNA blueprint can help map out a successful career.

The best time to do a general DNA assessment is when children are very young and begin to interact with each other in natural play. The earlier parents can observe their children's play conduct and inclinations, the more time is available to properly guide them toward beneficial educational and extracurricular choices.

Next, the early teen years constitute a critical point when youths should determine their Career DNA. This allows them time and opportunities to explore the careers matching their passions.

At any point in life, people can reexamine childhood interests and activities to evaluate personal strengths and their alignment with the ideal career path. It is never too late to do a Career DNA assessment.

Here are the key elements that define Career DNA:

Interests
Interests attract us to an activity that eventually turns into passion. Passion motivates us to do the best we can.

Aptitudes

Aptitudes are our natural born traits passed on to us through our genes. Our aptitudes allow us to succeed in what we are doing because we are using our strongest abilities. Skills are not aptitudes; rather they are learned tasks, which are mastered from practice. We can perform certain skills better than others because of our aptitudes.

Work Preferences

Preferences towards the types of tasks you perform each day include working with people, data, things, or ideas.

Personality Traits

The elements of our disposition are our personality traits. How we approach life and people influences the behavior of others, which in turn affects our ability to succeed.

Learning Styles

Learning styles are simply different approaches or ways of learning. People who are visual learn by seeing; those who are auditory learn by hearing, and those who are tactile/kinesthetic, learn by doing. Knowing your learning style will help you develop coping strategies to compensate for your weaknesses and capitalize on your strengths.

Multiple Intelligences

Conceived by Howard Gardner, multiple intelligences are seven different ways to demonstrate intellectual ability. Intelligences include: Visual/Spatial Intelligence, Verbal/Linguistic Intelligence, Logical/Mathematical Intelligence, Bodily/Kinesthetic Intelligence, Musical/Rhythmic Intelligence, Interpersonal Intelligence, and Intrapersonal Intelligence.

Values

Values are the elements which determine what, where, and how we want to live and work. If our career does not match our values, we may lose interest and not reach career success.

External Factors That Influence Our Career Decisions

The Career DNA components are the most important factors to consider in the career planning process. External influences such as economics and outside pressures should play a secondary role.

Economics

The need for financial support or gain is often a powerful factor in career decisions. Unfortunately, this is a factor that influences many of us to choose a specific career that may or may not be the right fit based on our Career DNA.

Outside Pressures

Pressures we receive from family and friends affect our career-making decisions. Those individuals who are not good decision makers or who have poor self-esteem are easily swayed and often allow others to make career decisions for them.

Factors at Different Age Groups

Ages 4–11 (Sarah and Chad)

At a young age, interests, aptitudes, and personality traits lead the way in making decisions that will affect career choices later in life. Children in this age group have no true economic concerns and have not been fully introduced to a value system. Outside pressures tend to be positive as parents and teachers encourage children to dream about careers. The toys and games children play can define their true interests. However, when assessing children's Career DNA, it is important not to confuse their natural desires with an activity they might engage in because of the external influences, such as interests of a parent or sibling. Their dynamic natural ability is shown in the choices they make independently.

Ages 12–18 (Ed and Bill)

As children move into adolescence, outside pressures begin to surface. Unfortunately, the other factors start to decrease significantly in the minds of the children in this group. Exploring careers that match aptitudes, interests, and personality traits can be overshadowed by the eagerness to mirror peer groups and to please parents' wishes. At this stage, we see behavior such as:

- the everyone-is-going-to-college syndrome
- interest in fashionable careers such as professional athletics, medicine, law, and law enforcement
- interest in careers prevalent on television
- the notion that making money is more important than contributing to society

Because they are in this age group, Bill and Ed's natural interests and aptitudes move into the background in favor of choosing cool careers. This environment, unfortunately, creates havoc when deciding upon a college major. Therefore, it is important for Paul and Amanda to discuss all the previously identified interests and natural talents when meeting with the children's counselors.

Ages 19–25

Economic concerns move to the top of decision-making factors as people begin college or trade careers. As the Holmes children are introduced to the reality of independence, they must ask themselves, "How are we going to support the lifestyle we are used to living?" If they fail to achieve financial independence, they will most likely move back home to live with their parents.

Unfortunately, individuals in this age group tend to use money and the assumed ease of earning a college degree as deciding factors in choosing a college major instead of choosing one based on their Career DNA. Because of peer or family pressures, many students target glamorous or high-paying careers. For example, the freshman college student declares he is a pre-med student. Soon he finds the rigorous course load to be overwhelming. Before the end of his sophomore year, his choice of major has changed to a less rigorous program. Again this second college major choice is not established from the student's interests, personality traits, aptitudes, and values, but rather the pressure of being able to graduate within four to six years.

Ages 26–55 (Paul and Amanda)

During this major portion of life, career choices can be overshadowed by the need to support ourselves financially. At this point, we are not thinking about the future or whether we will be happy in this career in ten years.

- How many young college grads have no intention of using their chosen degree? They have decided they want to be or do something else.
- How many people do we know who are in the wrong career?
- How many people do we know who are counting the days until retirement?
- How many people do we know who quit the career journey and jump from one job to another looking for the magical opportunity?

As a result of all they had learned, Paul and Amanda understood that they must make their career transitions using their true interests and natural abilities. To be truly happy and have fulfilling lives, they needed make sound personal decisions based on their overall self-assessments.

Ages 56+ (Retirement)

In our retirement years, we tend to make the full circle back to our childhood passions. We choose the activities that give us the most pleasure. We once again are drawn to activities very similar or related to the games we played as children.

- Those who played games outside when they were young now choose golf, sailing, or fishing as retirement activities.
- Those who loved to color, draw, and make crafts, may return to painting or ceramics.
- Those who loved to play board games now may sit for hours playing cards, chess, and bridge.
- Those who loved to play house or nurse choose to volunteer to help others.
- Those who started childhood businesses like the lemonade stands get involved in investment clubs and enjoy participating in passionate discussions about the stock market and investments.

For the Holmes's family, paying attention to everyday clues led them to an increased awareness of how each family member's Career DNA helps define appropriate career choices.

PART III

Making the Puzzle
Pieces Fit

8

Educational Building Blocks

Paul said, "I think Bill should take the most rigorous educational route to maximize the number of colleges that will accept him. And it would be wonderful if he could get a scholarship for either academic or athletic achievements." Amanda responded, "I agree that a scholarship would help us financially, but we can't forget about helping Bill match his interests to potential career choices."

Paul and Amanda realized they were entering the financial stress zone. How were they going to pay for Bill's college education? Would Bill be able to graduate in four years? Should he choose a college major before entering college or explore his options during his first two years of college? Would it make sense to devote eighty percent of his college life to playing a sport in exchange for an athletic scholarship? Would they be sending Bill off to college for an education to prepare him for a career and financial independence or to a glorified sports camp for fun and the chance to be a professional athlete? Amanda thought a bit and said, "We really need to understand how his education is affected if he selects an active sports program."

They met with his counselor to get some expert advice. She explained that planning the educational components of an individual's high school and college career should include foundation courses such as English, math, science, and social studies; courses that teach theory; courses that apply theory; and activities both inside and outside of school to help to explore and validate his interests, abilities, and career choices. She recommended that Bill create a blend of courses and activities during high school. He would need to master academic theory and apply it to the real world. In consideration of Bill's interest code (ERI) and in order to help clarify her recommendation, the counselor prepared the following chart for Bill:

BILL'S HIGH SCHOOL AND COLLEGE COURSE STRATEGY

ENTERPRISING

Business Courses: Accounting, Business Computer Applications, Business Law, Business Presentations, Career Planning, Co-op Work Experience, Desktop Publishing, Fashion Apparel and Accessories, Fashion Marketing, Financial Planning, Intro to Business, Marketing and Advertising, Sports Management, Sports Marketing, Wall Street I and II

Social Studies Courses: Anthropology, Criminal Justice, Economics, Holocaust, Law & Judicial Processes, Participating in Government, Practical Law, Psychology, Radio Broadcasting, Sociology, Trial Proceedings, Wars

Math Courses: Algebra, Calculus, Computer Science, Computers—Visual Basic, Geometry, Programming for the Web, Statistics, Trigonometry

Clubs: Freshmen Class Council, Investment Club, Junior Class Council, Model UN, Senior Class Council, Sophomore Class Council, DECA

Internships: Business owner, Government agency, Bank or financial company, Law office, Marketing company, Insurance company, Camp (event planner)

REALISTIC

Family Consumer Sciences Courses: Baking, Chef's Choice, International Foods

Career/Tech Center: Culinary Arts, Cosmetology

Technology Courses: Aerospace and Flight, Architecture Drawing, Automotive, Basic Electricity, Computer Networking, Construction Materials and Wood, Engineering, Graphic Communications, High Tech Computers, Small Engine Repair

Career/Tech Center: Auto Body Repair/Technology, Aviation Science/Aircraft Pilot, Carpentry, Computer Networking, Construction Electricity, Drafting/Computer Aided (CAD), Heating/Air Conditioning (HVAC), Horse Care, Horticulture/ Landscaping, Outdoor Equipment Technology, Veterinary Assisting, Welding

Health Courses: First Aid, CPR, Health, Sports Medicine

Clubs: Baseball Intramurals, Basketball Intramurals, Earth & Outdoors Club, Ecology Club, Indoor Soccer, Lacrosse Intramurals, Marine Biology Club, Robotics Club, Self Defense Club, Stage Crew,Technology Honor Society, Varsity Club, Volleyball Intramurals, Weight Training

Internships: Auto dealership, Construction company, Computer company, Civil or mechanical engineering firm, Architect, Security company, Manufacturing company, Landscaping company, Restaurant, Florist, Summer police, Fire department; Camp (sports leader)

INVESTIGATIVE

Science Courses: Biology, Chemistry, Earth Science, Environmental Science, Forensic Science, Marine Science, Physics

Career/Tech Center: Medical Assisting, Medical Laboratory, Nurse Assisting

English Courses: English 9, 10, 11, 12, British Literature, Creative Writing, Debating, Fundamentals of Acting, Journalism, Public Speaking, Shakespeare

Math Courses: Algebra, Calculus, Computer Science, Computers— Visual Basic, Geometry, Programming for the Web, Statistics, Trigonometry

Clubs: Biology Club, Chemistry Club, Chess Club, Earth Science Club, Journalism Club, Law Club, Math Science Technology Club, Literary Club, Physical Sciences Olympiad, Physics Olympiad, Science Olympiad

Internships: Hospital, Medical lab, Doctor's office, Veterinary office, Software company, Electrical or computer engineering firm, Environmental firm, Local newspaper, Camp (reading group)

While referring to this chart, Bill's counselor explained, "With this strong foundation, Bill will be able to identify a number of colleges that focus on several career options. Now let's discuss the college search process." She continued, "May I suggest you attend our annual Selecting a College event next week? We will be discussing the issues you need to consider as you explore Bill's postsecondary education options."

A week later, Paul, Amanda, and Bill attended the event. The first guest speaker spoke about the *Five Points to Consider in Choosing a College:*

"First you should discuss distance, costs, grade point average, and college admissions scores. You can narrow down your choices by looking at factors like college majors, career centers, alumni networks, types of students and campus environment, sports, and other leisure activities."

Here is what Paul, Amanda, and Bill were able to learn from the presentation:

Five Points to Consider in Choosing a Career

1. **College majors**—A college should have at least two majors Bill would consider. While visiting the college, they need to make sure to visit the academic departments to discuss course requirements and to view the accessible laboratory equipment.

2. **Career Centers**—They should visit the career center at each college. These centers should be able to supply a follow-up survey of the last graduating class, indicating where the graduates of each department obtained employment or admissions to graduate school and the job title and compensation offered to each student. They can check to see which organizations attend career fairs and actively recruit employees from this college and find out what other services are available for students. They should also find out if the center provides help in obtaining internships, writing resumes, and practicing for job interviews.

3. **Alumni Network**—They will need to determine the strength of the alumni network. Will this group be accessible to Bill? Will he be able to identify and contact an alumnus employed in his industry of choice? Does the career center work with the alumni center for finding employment for graduating students? They need to keep in mind that the purpose of obtaining a college education is to get a job!

4. **Types of students and campus environment**—Will Bill feel comfortable with the students at this college? Are the

living accommodations appropriate for him? Will he be able to live on campus for four years, or will he have to live off campus due to limited campus housing?

5. **Sports and other campus leisure activities**—What extra curricular activities does the campus offer? Clubs, academic competitions, intramural sports, divisional sport competition, etc.

"I really picked up some helpful advice from this speaker," Amanda said as she thumbed through the materials in their packets. "Let's make sure we have all the handouts to bring home. Okay, I see that the next presentation is going to be *Creating a Roadmap for Several Paths to Career Success*. Sounds interesting," Amanda added.

Creating a Roadmap for Several Paths to Career Success

The second speaker addressed the audience.

"Welcome, parents, students, and educators. I want to congratulate you on attending this event. It is never too early to discuss our children's future role in the workforce. We all want our children to be happy and successful with their choices. In order to improve the chances that they will be happy, we need to create a roadmap with several paths leading to appropriate career choices. As you know, there are many obstacles to success along any pathway. During our children's career route, they may be faced with insurmountable academic challenges; loss of college funds; unhappiness being away from home, family and, friends; turnover in coaches or changes affecting the university's financial commitment to a team; or poor choices due to a lack of self-assessment before choosing a college and major.

"If our children meet with any of these challenges, they need to have a backup plan to pursue without losing too much of the investment. By this, I mean, I encourage all of you tonight to sit down and discuss alternative routes to career success.

"If your child is contemplating two separate career choices based on self-assessment activities, then you need to complete a second roadmap. It is most important that the family be aware of the child's choices, alternate paths, and the entire cost of achieving the educational goal.

"Every successful business develops a business plan. The company identifies goals, targets, procedures on how to reach the goals, and proposed expenditures. In purchasing a home, each family will create a financial plan of action taking into consideration the purchase price of the home and the necessary steps it may take to remodel and expand the structure. The same type of planning ahead is necessary for choosing and financing your educational road trip to career success!

"To illustrate a career roadmap, let's assume your child wants to pursue a career in the health field. Maybe she has been talking about becoming a doctor. This is a wonderful goal, but your child needs to be prepared to choose alternate paths. You can use our sample roadmap for health field career chart as an example of how several plans can be considered within a chosen career field."

Sample Roadmap for Health Field Career

Plan	Years of Education/ Degree Level	Careers	Estimated Total Cost* (Public To Private Institution)
A	College: • 5 – 8 Years • B.S. (Bachelor of Science) plus professional degree	• Pharmacist, Dentist • Physical and Occupational Therapist • Physical Therapist • Physician's Assistant • Psychiatrist • Psychologist • Speech Therapist	$120,000 – $280,000
B	Military/College: • 5 – 8 Years • B.S. plus professional degree • Enlisted officer in the armed services	• Dentist • Dietitian • Optometrist • Pharmacist • Physical and Occupational Therapist • Physician Assistant • Physician or Surgeon • Psychologist • Registered Nurse • Speech Therapist	$0 as a ROTC military student enrolled in college A five-year commitment to armed services after receiving a professional degree
C	College: • 4 – 5 Years • B.S. (Bachelor of Science)	• Dietitian • Medical Laboratory Scientist • Optometrist • Registered Nurse	$60,000 – $140,000

Plan	Years of Education/ Degree Level	Careers	Estimated Total Cost* (Public To Private Institution)
D	Community College: • 2 Years • A.A.S. (Associate in Applied Science)	• Medical Lab Assistant • Nurse • Occupational Therapist • Respiratory Assistant • X-Ray Technician	$8,000 – $10,000
E	Military: • 3 Years Commitment • High School Diploma • Military Training	• Cardiopulmonary and EEG Technician • Dental and Optical Laboratory Technician • Dental Specialist • Medical Care Technician • Medical Laboratory Technician • Medical Record Technician • Medical Service Technician • Optometric Technician • Pharmacy Technician • Physical and Occupational Therapy Specialist • Radiology (X-Ray) Technician	$0 A three-year commitment to armed services is required
F	No College: • High School Diploma • Additional on the job or technical school training	• Hospital Transporter • Medical Office Clerk • Medical Records Clerk • Phlebotomist	$0 – $10,000

*Calculations assume $15,000 per year for public institutions and $35,000 per year for private institutions. These estimated costs include room and board.

Paul sat back and felt dazed by all this information. "I never really thought about the time and effort we must put into our children's careers," he sighed. "We have a good deal to think about. We need to go back over Bill's self-assessment to make sure we're on the right track for his career success."

Amanda added, "I don't want Bill to complete six years of college and then tell us he is not happy with his choice. We are talking about spending $150,000 for his education. Do we want to saddle him with student loans? I agree with you, Paul. We need to create several plans of action for Bill and the other children."

It had been a long evening, but Paul, Amanda, and Bill learned a great deal about how much time and effort families should put into selecting postsecondary education options for their children.

Paul sighed. "Education has become so expensive; we really can't afford to make quick decisions. We need to take advantage of all the expert advice that is available and dedicate the time it will take to make the best decisions. Let's sleep on it tonight and get a fresh start tomorrow."

9

Creative Ways to Win
the Career Game

Several times a year, the local high school hosted career events for students and their parents. One event, titled *Alternative Paths to Career Success*, was particularly popular each year. Since parents today tend to focus on college as the *only* path to career success, they may not consider other options. In reality, college is not necessarily the best path to career success for every student. When Paul and Amanda met with Ed's counselor, she suggested that Ed might want to consider some alternative options. She advised the Holmes family to attend the upcoming *Alternative Paths to Career Success* event.

The event turned out to be even better than the family expected, and it opened their eyes to the variety of options available to students as they graduate from high school. The evening began with a kick-off presentation delivered by the guidance department. The counselors explained that a college degree was not the only route to career success. This program was designed to give students and parents a chance to hear about those other pathways and to speak to the experts about these options.

Some parents voiced concerns since they had always wanted their children to graduate from college. The counselors approached this subject with a great deal of sensitivity, explaining how their experience had shown that a college degree was not the only way to a successful career and fulfilling life. They also stressed that all students should focus on selecting a learning environment in which they could excel. The overall message for the evening was that there are plenty of other options students, and their parents should consider before thinking college is the only way to go. The counselors then encouraged all the parents and students to take full advantage of the seminars during the evening. At the end of the event, each student would have an opportunity to schedule appointments with their counselors to discuss their individual situation before making a final decision.

Paul said, "Boy have we got our work cut out for us! Take a look at this program listing all the seminars being offered here."

Amanda said, "We should pick a few seminars that seem most appropriate for Ed." She thought for a moment. "We know Ed can't stand being in a class and would rather be outside on a ball field or learning something hands-on. She turned to Ed and said, "Here are the seminars to choose from, Ed. Which ones do you think you would benefit from?"

Career Seminar Selections

SEMINAR TOPIC 1: **Stepping Out to Full-Time Employment**
What should you look for in a full-time employment opportunity?
- Training—formal or informal
- Legal employment, which brings workers compensation and record of employment
- Medical Benefits
- Tuition reimbursement

SEMINAR TOPIC 2: **Apprenticeship Training and Union Sponsorship**

- Review training contract
- Review career paths and pay scales
- Identify location of on-the-job training
- Clarify when classroom training takes place

SEMINAR TOPIC 3: **Careers via the Military**

- ASVAB entrance exam
- Choice of military service
- Choice of career paths for enlisted personnel
- Choice of career paths for officers
- How does training in the military differ from an education in a college classroom?
- Obtaining a two- or four-year college degree while in the service

SEMINAR TOPIC 4: **Work for the Government**

- Entry-level civil service jobs are available at the town, county, state, and federal levels
- Must take entrance exam
- Benefits—medical, dental, and tuition reimbursement
- Job security
- Move about the country in a federal position

SEMINAR TOPIC 5: **Temporary Employment Agencies**

- Opportunity to try different jobs and industries without making a commitment
- In-house training on computers
- Good connections to help with future decisions

SEMINAR TOPIC 6: **One-Year Certificate Programs for Career Focused Education**

- One-year programs from colleges or technical schools
- Offering specialized certificates to train quickly and efficiently for specific occupations, like driver training, retail management, drafting, fire investigation, HVAC, help desk, information technology, and paralegal studies
- Direct placement
- Competitive pay scale

SEMINAR TOPIC 7: **Online Education and Distance Learning**

- Two- and four-year degrees available
- Online learning—learning through the computer
- Distance Learning—learning through television
- Credit for real-life experiences

Ed scanned the list and said, "Well, I guess I am interested in hearing more about apprenticeships, the military, and working for the government." He and his parents set off with a game plan to attend those three seminars. They found all three interesting and collected a lot of information. On the way home, Ed seemed most interested in an apprenticeship with a union.

That night, before falling asleep, Amanda said to Paul, "I'm so glad we didn't assume Ed should go to college just because other parents are so focused on getting their children into the best schools. We are really letting him take an active role in deciding what choice is best for him. I think that is the way to guide him toward success—his way."

Paul replied, "You're right. He's got his own interests and strengths, and the most important thing is that he chooses a path that will make him happy. I know success will follow that happiness."

10

Solving the Grad School Puzzle

"I don't want to complicate things even more," Amanda sighed, "but I'm wondering if we should be thinking about whether or not grad school will be necessary for the kids, based on their career choices."

For Sarah, the answer was simple, to reach her goal and land a lucrative job at NASA, she would need a graduate degree. She viewed graduate school as adding extra polish to her undergraduate education. Some of the questions she pondered while she was working on her bachelor's degree in physics were whether to get some industry experience in between undergraduate and graduate school and what type of graduate degree to pursue.

Late in her junior year, she made an appointment with a counselor at the career center on campus. The counselor spent some time discussing Sarah's dreams and career aspirations. She explained that graduate school is not exploratory in nature. The counselor emphasized, "Those who go on to graduate school should already know what they want. And they are pursuing their graduate degree to become an expert in their field."

The counselor felt that Sarah was a strong candidate for graduate school and, with her high grade point average and participation in numerous clubs and organizations, she should apply to top schools such as MIT (Massachusetts Institute of Technology). The counselor suggested that Sarah use her membership club contacts to meet someone who had worked at NASA. She felt that having this kind of contact would give her insight into whether or not she should go straight to graduate school or take time off to work in the aviation or aeronautics fields first.

As it turns out, one of Sarah's math professors had worked at NASA for a number of years. She made an appointment to meet with him during office hours. He was extremely helpful and gave her the names of two scientists who were still working at the agency. He offered to contact each of them and introduce Sarah so that she could spend a while talking with them about her plans for the future and get their recommendations about graduate school.

The opportunity to speak with both of these scientists excited Sarah. They invited her to visit their facility where she would meet with them and tour the various departments. This became a turning point in her life. She met a number of key scientists, learned about some of the work they were doing, and received advice on how to proceed with her education. Through her contacts at NASA, Sarah landed a contract position that would give her first-hand experience at the agency. This, in turn, would help her to determine exactly where she would like to work at NASA. She could select a grad school program to help her to prepare for her future.

One of Sarah's friends from college had quite a different experience. Rebecca was a good student, majoring in liberal arts, but was having some difficulties making up her mind about what she wanted to do after college. She had thought about becoming a lawyer but felt that she did not have enough information to make a good decision. Her counselor advised her to apply for internships for the summer between her junior and senior years. Rebecca was able to make some connections at an internship fair on campus. She lined up interviews at two law firms, prepared well for her interviews, and ended up with offers from both companies. She decided to go with a medium-sized law firm located not too far from her parents' home.

Over that summer, Rebecca learned a great deal about what life is like in a law firm. Unfortunately, she could not get excited about the work. She found it tedious and methodical.

She called up Sarah one evening and said, "I am so glad that I took this internship. I've realized that being a lawyer just is not for me."

"Better to know that now," said Sarah. "Imagine if you had taken the LSATs and started at a law school? This way, you have a moment or two to think about your options."

Sarah shared how her family had benefited from determining their interest codes after reviewing their favorite activities as children. "It made choosing a career pretty easy, overall. You should go back to the career center and find out about your Holland Code. By the way," Sarah added, "what did you play with as a child?"

Rebecca replied, "I always loved to play with dolls."

"What else?" Sarah asked.

Rebecca started to smile and said, "Well, don't laugh, but I used to pretend that I was a teacher and the dolls were my students."

"Aha," Sarah replied, "I bet the first letter of your interest code is S for social!"

Rebecca asked, "What exactly does *that* mean?"

Sarah explained, "It just means that you are social; people who fall into this category like to help other people."

"So I guess my wanting to be a lawyer wasn't that far off."

"You're right," Sarah said. "Why don't you go to the career center and do the assessment with your counselor?"

"I'm on it," Rebecca shot back.

A couple of weeks later, Sarah ran into Rebecca on campus and asked her how her assessment went.

"It turns out; my interest code is SAR—Social, Artistic, and Realistic." Rebecca said proudly. "And guess what? I did some extensive research about careers, and I think I found one I will love."

"What did you come up with?" Sarah asked impatiently.

"A kindergarten teacher!"

"How about that!" Sarah exclaimed. "So playing teacher with your dolls was a pretty big clue!" She laughed. It seemed like Rebecca had found her calling.

Even though Rebecca had a very good feeling that teaching was the right career for her, she wanted to make sure it was before wasting time and money going down the wrong path. She had heard a new daycare center had just opened in town, so she applied for a summer position. She loved being with the children. It invigorated her, inspired her, and well before the end of that summer, she knew she had found her calling. She ended up applying for grad school and majored in early childhood education.

11

Reaching the Finish Line
to Capture the Prize

Let's fast forward to the warm June night at the beginning of the story when the Holmes family was celebrating all of their successful career choices. At that point, each member of the family benefited from everything Paul learned during his career transition. He and Amanda learned just how critical career plans can be. Paul thought about how closely he had worked with his career counselor and about all the research he had done on potential careers for someone who is investigative, conventional, and enterprising.

"Until that point in my life, I had never thought of starting my own business," he reflected.

His research and work with his counselor, Maggie, convinced him that although the enterprising part of his personality had not been in the forefront over the years, he definitely had an interest in running his own business. Why not? The fact that he was investigative, conventional, and enterprising indicated that he had the interest and skills necessary to be analytical and to solve complex problems, to organize anything he put his mind to, and to run a successful business.

"Now I have my own thriving company!" Paul exclaimed.

Paul recognized how much he enjoyed running his business, which specialized in providing payroll solutions for small- to medium-sized companies. He drew upon his extensive experience as a software programmer to design an innovative and cost-effective payroll processing program. It turns out that his ability to organize things complemented his technical programming skills. This enabled him to develop a well-designed program that could effectively meet the stringent requirements of payroll systems.

Paul laughed and said, "If I had never been laid off from the software company, I probably would have never heard about the Holland Interest Inventory." He realized that without all he had learned about himself by completing the assessment with his counselor, he may not have had the inspiration or self-awareness necessary to launch his own business. And he would not have been able to take what he had learned from his experience and help his whole family plan career paths using this simple, yet powerful technique.

Along the way, Paul, Amanda, and their children learned so much about their potential and became more confident in their individual abilities. This innovative theory demonstrates how the games we loved to play as children can be strong indicators of key interests and potential career paths. It turned into a rewarding adventure for the entire family.

Amanda worked at the local art supply store as a part-time salesclerk for several years. At that point, she felt it was the right time for her to have her own store. She signed up for workshops on starting a business at the local Small Business Administration office. There, she learned about the importance of having a business plan. She also learned about marketing, accounting, and basic business operations. She kept her eyes open for an available storefront with a good location for an art supply business. It took about six months, but she finally found a good-sized storefront in a nearby town.

It was a college town and there were always art students in need of supplies. This factored strongly into Amanda's business plan. With support from Paul and the children, she opened the shop just as a new freshman class was starting at the college. It took a while for Amanda to break even, since she had invested a good deal of money in the extensive inventory she needed. Her business gradually grew, and she found that she loved many aspects of running her own business. She also loved helping college students with their projects, which were often shared with Amanda upon completion. She even kept a portfolio with pictures of the students' finished artwork. She thrived in this environment!

After graduating from college, Bill became a mechanical engineer and worked for a major car manufacturer. Given all we've learned about the games he played as a child and his interest code of ERI—Enterprising, Realistic and Investigative, this is no surprise. What about the other children? How did their education and career paths unfold?

Ed completed high school and played baseball while attending college. He continued to play ball for a few years after he received his associate's degree in criminal justice. If you remember, his interest code was RSC—Realistic, Social, and Conventional. Ed really wanted to play professional ball but followed his high school counselor's advice and had a backup plan since professional sports careers can be extremely difficult to land, and are often short-lived. He decided to become a police officer. This allowed him to continue to play ball during college, then to transition into a fulfilling career in the local police force. But he never gave up coaching. He spent several hours each week coaching local children through the Police Athletic League (PAL).

While she was still quite young, Sarah entered a job-shadowing program that had started within the school district. This gave her the chance to visit the local companies' laboratories to meet the research scientists and to learn about their jobs. Sarah received her undergraduate degree in physics and a master's degree in aeronautics. She took a job at NASA, managing a team of research scientists. Her interest code was IRS—Investigative, Realistic, and Social. Remembering the nights she stayed up late peering into space through her telescope, Sarah smiled and realized how those interests from so long ago remained strong.

Not surprisingly, Chad took a very different path. With an interest code of CRE—Conventional, Realistic, and Enterprising—Chad decided to major in accounting and got his CPA certificate. He started to specialize in working with small business owners. When he was younger, even though many of the other children his age did not share his love for organizing things, that's what made him happy. He was grateful that his parents had the foresight to share the secrets of their own midlife career explorations with him and his siblings, allowing them to find truly fulfilling careers. He knew that when he had children of his own, he would not only notice what they played with, but he would encourage them to explore those interests throughout their lives.

Although each member of the family had a different interest code, you may have noticed some common themes among them. Enterprising, which was shared by five members of the family, was a common thread highlighting the fact that interests and abilities could pass on from parents to their children. The seemingly unlimited career possibilities for each interest code combination amazed Paul.

Throughout his life, he shared his career exploration experience with friends, colleagues, and relatives. He inspired others to think back to when they were children and to remember the games they loved to play. He encouraged them to complete the quick assessment to determine their interest code. Next, he suggested they compare the results to their childhood play preferences, games, and activities. More often than not, they were able to accurately connect their true interests to their childhood play habits. This validation often led them to investigate their complete Career DNA with a consultant.

Repeatedly, Paul heard from friends, relatives, and business acquaintances that reflecting on their childhood activities, along with completing formal assessments, helped them find more fulfilling careers. One of the things he learned was that most adults change careers more than five times over the span of their working years. It was apparent to him that understanding your Career DNA can be useful throughout one's entire life.

Paul thought, "You are never too old to revisit your childhood!"

PART IV

The Career Planning Process

12

Rules of the Game

In playing chess, like any other game, each player begins with a goal to win. Although winning may be the objective, it is a player's knowledge, experience, and approach in each move that make it an exciting journey toward victory. You could say it is much the same when you set out to play the career game. Attaining a satisfying career is not a one-step process, but rather an exhilarating journey to be taken over a number of years. As in chess, we must continually consider and validate choices along the way. When playing the career game, it is essential to recognize our individual strengths and abilities, and to be as strategic as the chess player when making every move. If those choices bring career success and happiness, then we made the right moves. However, if we find that those career choices were not suitable, then an alternative tactical career move is required. Therefore, every player in the career game should always have at least two, if not more, career plan strategies.

It is said that in the twenty-first century, workers will, on average, change jobs within one or two career clusters, five to ten times. This represents a significant shift from the reality throughout most of the twentieth century, when many workers chose a single job path within a career and remained with one or two employers for thirty or more years. In today's modern world, career seekers find a new challenge. Fifty years ago, there were a limited number of careers and career names. Now there are new job titles and career clusters emerging in the workforce to prepare for an ever-evolving, quick-paced job market that demands highly skilled, adaptable workers. One can compare career choices from years ago to choosing a crayon from a box of twenty-four colors. Nowadays a box of crayons contains five hundred blended colors—many more possibilities for the individual trying to make the right career choices.

With all this in mind, as you embark on playing the career game, begin the planning process by following these fundamental rules of the game:

1. Always start with self-assessment. You can make solid career decisions based on your Career DNA. First, identify your authentic interests, aptitudes, work preferences, personality traits, learning styles, multiple intelligences, and values. A good career counselor will be able to take all these DNA indicators and guide you toward appropriate career choices within career clusters.

2. Build a strong foundation. Next, build a strong educational foundation while exploring career choices. This will lead to sound decisions when choosing high school courses and eventually, a college major. As a high school student, you should choose academic courses as well as career and technical education courses. Academic subjects, such as English, math, science, and social studies, build a solid knowledge base. Career and technical courses, such as business and technology, apply that knowledge base to real-world scenarios.

3. Validate career choices. During the high school and college years, the most effective way to validate your career choices is to participate in clubs, sports, and other activities, which help you to develop skills such as teamwork, negotiation, persuasion, problem solving, and multitasking. At the moment, most schools offer out-of-school experiences like shadowing career professionals, supervised non-paid internships, and paid work experiences. By the time you graduate from high school and college, you should have experienced all three of these activities. Today's employers are calling for two internships related to the corporation's mission and your college major.

4. Plan the next level of training and education. The twenty-first–century world is demanding additional training and education after completion of high school, which can be obtained at a postsecondary college, in the military, or through on-the-job training by the employer. Armed with Career DNA, a strong educational foundation, and out-of school experiences, you'll be prepared to choose an appropriate career path.

5. No longer should a high school student say, "I don't know what I want to study in college." You should feel confident to say, "I know the best career choices for me are the following two paths..." Begin your next move in the career game with a Plan A and several backup plans. A minimum of two related career plans will allow you to make any appropriate changes if you realize Plan A is not your ideal option after all.

6. Choose an industry and identify employers. Ask two final questions in the career planning process: *Which industries are ideal for me, and which employers should I target?* For example, if you were to choose the accounting career path, you need to decide which industry would best suit you. An

accountant could work in a variety of industries such as hospitality, entertainment, banking, health care, or education. Within each industry a job will differ as to work environment, days and hours representing the work schedule, amount of travel, specific tasks, career ladders, and earnings, to name just a few. Match your work preferences and life values to the appropriate industry. The most effective way to accomplish this is to experience a variety of internships and summer jobs. Many times a young person will return to the same camp-counseling job each summer because the choice is convenient. The ideal situation would be to find a new summer job each year which relates to your college major. It is very possible that internships will lead to full-time employment opportunities.

Once you have identified desirable industries, the last move is to identify several employers within each industry. Participation in job fairs, career days, career-related clubs, and professional trade associations will help you to determine which employers to target.

Making successful career choices may be a game of strategy, but the challenges can be rewarding when you know *how* to play. Before you begin, seek out a career counselor that is well-versed in the game. A career counselor is like a game master who can navigate you through all your career moves—from discovering your Career DNA to exploring childhood interests to determining appropriate educational courses, to creating a winning game plan to finding the perfect job. You will find that the one difference in the career game over playing chess is that every player can be a winner!

PART V

Connecting
Games to Careers

13

Career DNA Synopsis by Interest Group

REALISTIC – The Doers

INVESTIGATIVE – The Thinkers

ARTISTIC – The Creators

SOCIAL – The Helpers

ENTERPRISING – The Persuaders

CONVENTIONAL – The Organizers

The following charts offer a snapshot of how each interest group correlates with particular types of games, toys or activities of interest, which are also directly related to the suggested high school courses, clubs, internships, 2-year college majors, 4-year college majors and sample professions.

REALISTIC—The Doers

Games/Toys/ Activities of Interest	Suggested High School Courses	Suggested High School Club Focus
• Action-oriented video and computer games • Being physically active • Building blocks, models, woodworking • Building things, using hands • Computer software downloading and hardware savvy • Hunting and fishing • Landscaping, growing plants and flowers • Playing sports, coaching teams • Playing with radio controlled toys, trucks, and action figures • Refinishing furniture • Repairing cars and equipment • Taking exercise classes • Target shooting • Tinkering with machines, vehicles • Toy tool and building sets • Working on electronic equipment • Working outdoors	**FAMILY CONSUMER SCIENCES** • Baking • Chef's Choice • International Foods **HEALTH** • First Aid, CPR • Health Sports Medicine **CAREER/TECH CENTER** • Culinary Arts • Cosmetology **TECHNOLOGY** • Aerospace and Flight • Architecture Drawing • Automotive • Basic Electricity • Computer Networking • Construction Materials and Wood • Engineering • Graphic Communications • High Tech Computers • Small Engine Repair **CAREER/TECH CENTER** • Auto Body Repair/Technology • Aviation Science/Aircraft Pilot • Carpentry • Computer Networking • Construction Electricity • Drafting/Computer Aided (CAD) • Heating/Air Conditioning (HVAC) • Horse Care • Horticulture/Landscaping • Outdoor Equipment Technology • Veterinary Assisting • Welding	• Baseball Intramurals • Basketball Intramurals • Earth & Outdoors Club • Ecology Club • Indoor Soccer • Lacrosse Intramurals • Marine Biology Club • Robotics Club • Self Defense Club • Stage Crew • Technology Honor Society • Varsity Club • Volleyball Intramurals • Weight Training

Internship Options	2-Year College Majors	4-Year College Majors
• Architectural firm • Auto dealership • Camp—sports leader • Civil or Mechanical Engineering firm • Computer company • Construction company • Fire Department Volunteer • Florist • Hotel Clerk • Landscaping company • Manufacturing company • Restaurant • Security company • Summer Police Academy • Restaurant Management	• Automotive Service Specialist • Computer Science • Computer Technology • Criminal Justice: Police Option • Engineering & Technology • Architectural or Construction Technology • Fire Protection Technology • Fitness Specialist • Horticulture: Floriculture Option • Landscape Development • Manufacturing • Physical Therapist Assistant	• Architectural Technology • Civil Engineering Technology • Computer Network Administration • Computer Software Specialist • Construction • Drafting & Design Technology • Electrical Engineering Technology • Electronics Engineering Technology • Engineering Technology • Law Enforcement Technology • Mechanical Engineering Technology • Supply Chain Management

Sample of Professions

• Computer Technician • Cook or Chef • Dental Assistant	• Electrical Engineer • Food Service Providers • Laboratory Technician	• Mechanical Engineer • Oceanographer • Optician

Realistic, or the Doers, are people who usually have athletic or mechanical ability, prefer to work with objects, machines, tools, plants or animals, or to be outdoors.

INVESTIGATIVE—The Thinkers

Games/Toys/ Activities of Interest	Suggested High School Courses	Suggested High School Club Focus
• Analytical video games • Belonging to a book club • Collecting rocks, stamps, coins, or other related items • Interpreting formulas • Lab experiments • Playing with amateur radio • Reading scientific or technology journals • Researching projects • Solving crossword puzzles • Solving math problems • Using a microscope, magnifier, chemistry set, or stethoscope • Using computers • Visiting museums	**SCIENCE** • Biology • Chemistry • Earth Science • Environmental Science • Forensic Science • Marine Science • Physics **CAREER/TECH CENTER** • Medical Assisting • Medical Laboratory • Nurse Assisting **ENGLISH** • American and British Literature • Creative Writing • Debating • English 9, 10, 11, 12 • Fundamentals of Acting • Journalism • Public Speaking • Shakespeare **MATH** • Algebra, Geometry • Calculus • Computer Science • Computers: Visual Basic • Programming for the Web • Statistics • Trigonometry	• Biology Club • Chemistry Club • Chess Club • Earth Science Club • Journalism Club • Law Club • Math Science Technology Club • Literary Club • Physical Sciences Olympiad • Physics Olympiad • Science Olympiad

Investigative, or the Thinkers, are people who like to observe, learn, investigate, analyze, evaluate, or solve problems.

Internship Options	2-Year College Majors	4-Year College Majors
• Camp—reading group • Doctor's office • Engineering firm—electrical or computer • Environmental firm • Government research • Hospital • Medical lab • Software company • Veterinary office	• Aero, Civil, and Mechanical Engineering Sequence • American Sign Language • Chemical Engineering • Dietetic Technician • Electrical Engineering Technology • Health Information Technology • Interpreter American Sign Language Sequence for the Deaf • Medical Assistant • Nursing • Occupational Therapy Assistant • Ophthalmic Dispensing • Psychology: Liberal Studies • Science Laboratory Technology • Software Specialist • Veterinary Science Technology	• Anthropology • Bioengineering • Biology • Cardiovascular Technology • Chemical Engineering • Chemical Technology • Chemistry • Civil Engineering • Computer Science & Engineering • Economics • Electrical Engineering • Engineering Physics • Environmental Sciences or Studies • Geography & Planning • Geology • Industrial Engineering Technology • International Studies • Linguistics • Math Education • Mathematics & Computer Science Education • Medical Assisting Technology • Pharmacy • Physics • Pre-Dentistry • Pre-Medicine • Pre-Veterinary Medicine • Sociology

Sample of Professions

• Anthropologist • Archeologist • Biologist • Chemist	• Computer Programmer • Doctor • Economist • Health care provider	• Market Research Analyst • Pharmacist • Veterinarian

ARTISTIC—The Creators

Games/Toys/ Activities of Interest	Suggested High School Courses	Suggested High School Club Focus
• Attend concerts, theatres, and art exhibits • Computer programs geared for design, art, and digital photography • Designing fashions, interiors, or sets for plays • Playing a musical instrument • Reading fiction, poetry, or plays • Singing, acting, or dancing • Sketching, drawing, painting, or creating homemade crafts • Taking photographs • Traveling, speaking foreign languages • Visiting art museums • Writing stories, poetry, music	**ART** • Advertising Design 1 and 2 • Cartooning • Ceramics • Drawing 1 and 2 • Fashion Illustration • Film History and Critique • Filmmaking • Media Arts • Painting 1 and 2 • Photography • Sculpture • Studio in Art • Studio in Crafts • Studio in Great Artists • Video Portfolio • Video Production **CAREER/TECH CENTER** • Advertising Art • Fashion Merchandising/Design • Floral Arts • Photography • Printing • Video Production **MUSIC** • Concert Band • Concert Choir • Orchestra • Symphonic Band • Theory of Music **SECOND LANGUAGE** • American Sign Language I and II • French • German • Italian • Spanish **ENGLISH** • American and British Literature • Creative Writing • Debating • English 9, 10, 11, 12 • Fundamentals of Acting • Journalism • Public Speaking • Shakespeare	• Art Club • Brass Quintet • Chamber Music/ Fiddle Club • Creative Spotlight • Dancing • German Honor Society • Italian Club/Honor Society • Jazz Band • Living Theater 2000 • Magic: The Gathering • National Art Honor Society • National French Honor Society • National Media Arts H. S. • Photography Club • Show Choir • Spanish Honor Society • Stage Band • Thespian Troupe 2035 • Tournament of Plays • Winter Drama Producer/Director

Internship Options	2-Year College Majors	4-Year College Majors
• Advertising firm • Art gallery • Art supply store • Camp—arts, crafts, or drama group • Film or video company • Local newspaper art/layout department • Museum • Sign company • Theatre or dance group	• Communications and Media Arts • Fine Arts • Graphic Design • Interior Design • Journalism • Performing Arts: Drama • Performing Arts: Music • Photographic Imaging • Radio and Television Production • Technical Communication	• Art • Art Education • Art History • Dance • English • English Education • Film/Video • Foreign Language Education • Humanities • Library-Media Education • Music • Music Education • Philosophy • Theatre
Sample of Professions		
• Architect • Choreographer • Clothing Designer	• Graphic Designer • Interior Decorator • Medical Illustrator	• Photographer • Web Designer • Writer/Editor

Artistic, or the Creators, are people who have artistic, innovative, or intuitional abilities and like to work in unstructured situations using their imagination and creativity.

SOCIAL—The Helpers

Games/Toys/ Activities of Interest	Suggested High School Courses	Suggested High School Club Focus
• Attending sporting events • Active in Girl or Boy Scouts • Caring for children • Communications • Cooperating well with others • Going to parties or meeting new friends • Helping others with personal concerns • Joining campus or community organizations • Leading a group discussion • Mediating disputes • Planning and supervising activities • Playing school or tea party. • Playing team sports • Playing with dolls or stuffed animals • Religious activities • Teaching or training others • Text messaging, e-mailing, participating in Internet forums, virtual networking • Volunteering with social action groups • Writing letters	**BUSINESS** • Accounting • Business Law • Business Presentations • Career Planning • Fashion Apparel and Accessories • Fashion Marketing • Financial Planning • Intro to Business • Marketing and Advertising • Sports Management • Sports Marketing • Wall Street I and II **SOCIAL STUDIES** • Anthropology • Criminal Justice • Economics • Holocaust • Law & Judicial Processes • Participating in Government • Practical Law • Psychology **CAREER/TECH CENTER** • Early Childhood Education & Care • Travel & Tourism • Radio Broadcasting • Sociology • Trial Proceedings • Wars **FAMILY CONSUMER SCIENCES** • Child Development • Early Childhood and Nursing • Interior Decorating • Parenting • Relationships	• Debating Team • DECA • General Student Association • Habitat for Humanity • HIV Peer Educators' Club • Interact • Key Club • Multicultural Club • On Target/Positive Edge • Radio Broadcasting • Renaissance Club • S.A.D.D. • School of Business

Social, or the Helpers, are people who like to work with other people to enlighten, inform, help, train, or cure them, or are skilled with words.

Internship Options	2-Year College Majors	4-Year College Majors
• Camp—counselor • Child care or school • Community relations department • Human resources department • Reception • Retail sales store	• Chemical Dependency Counseling • Community Service Assistant • Community/Outdoor Recreation • Early Childhood Education Exercise Studies • Human Resources Management Sequence • Recreation Leadership Sociology • Therapeutic Recreation Sequence • Travel & Tourism	• Anthropology • American Studies • Athletic Training • Career & Technical Education • Community Health Education • Correctional Technology • Criminal Justice • Elementary Education • Emergency Medical Science Technology • Health & Human Performance Education • European Studies • History • Institutional Health Care • International Relations • Kinesiotherapy • Latin American Studies • Law & Social Thought • Middle East Studies • Mental Health Technology • Physical Education • Physical Therapy • Political Science & Public Administration • Psychology • Public Administration • Recreation/Leisure Studies • Science Education • Social Service • Social Studies Education • Social Work • Speech Language Pathology • Special Education • Therapeutic Recreation

Sample of Professions

• Counselor • Fitness Instructor • Hospital Administrator	• Life Coach • Physical Therapist • Police Officer Social Worker	• Teacher, College Professor • Social Worker • Teacher, College Professor

ENTERPRISING—The Persuaders

Games/Toys/ Activities of Interest	Suggested High School Courses	Suggested High School Club Focus
• Buying or collecting items to resell for a profit • Computer games or Web sites oriented toward money, buying and selling, business ownership, Internet companies, stocks, or purchase pricing • Doing jobs around the house or neighborhood to earn money such as babysitting, yard work, or having a paper route • Leadership roles such as running a youth group, high-ranked Scouting, or coordinating play activities • Making decisions for others on what to play or where to have fun • Playing board games such as chess, checkers or Monopoly • Playing lemonade stand, grocery store or bank • Raising money or selling items for charity • Reading business journals • Selling products to earn top recognition such as cookies, candy bars, or wrapping paper • Setting up and running a carwash • Watching the stock market	**BUSINESS** • Accounting • Business Computer Apps. • Business Law • Business Presentations • Career Planning • Cooperative Work Experience • Desktop Publishing • Fashion Apparel and Accessories • Fashion Marketing • Financial Planning • Intro to Business • Marketing and Advertising • Sports Management • Sports Marketing • Wall Street I and II **SOCIAL STUDIES** • Anthropology • Criminal Justice • Economics • Holocaust • Law & Judicial Processes • Participating in Government • Practical Law • Psychology • Radio Broadcasting • Sociology • Trial Proceedings • Wars **MATH** • Algebra • Calculus • Computer Science • Computers: Visual Basic • Geometry • Programming for the Web • Statistics • Trigonometry	• DECA • Freshman Class Council • Investment Club • Junior Class Council • Model UN • Senior Class Council • Sophomore Class Council

Internship Options	2-Year College Majors	4-Year College Majors
• Bank or financial company • Business owner • Camp—event planner • Government agency • Insurance company • Law office • Marketing company	• Accounting • Business Administration • Banking • Finance • Insurance • Management • Marketing • Office • Real Estate • Business Management • Management • Office • Restaurant • Retail Business	• Business Administration • Business Management Technology • Electronic Commerce • Entrepreneurship/Family & Small Business • Finance • Human Resource Management Industrial Engineering • International Business • Management • Marketing • Marketing & Sales Technology • Operations Management • Organizational Development Management • Pre-Law • Professional Sales • Public Affairs & Community Services • Purchasing • Real Estate Technology • Urban Studies

Sample of Professions		
• Account Executive • Advertising/Marketing Manager • Bank Manager	• Elected Government Official • Entrepreneur • Investment Manager • Lawyer	• Office Manager • Real Estate Associate • Sales Manager

Enterprising, or the Persuaders, are people who like to work with people, influencing, persuading, performing, leading, or managing for organizational goals or economic gain.

CONVENTIONAL—The Organizers

Games/Toys/ Activities of Interest	Suggested High School Courses	Suggested High School Club Focus
• Arranging and sorting items by category such as toys, games, magazines, trophies, music, or movies • Collecting things like dolls, baseball cards, stamps, or coins • Computer programs related to data recall, organizing, scheduling, recording, and documenting • Household chores like organizing a closet, the garage, or basement. • Keeping club or family records • Keeping score playing games • Organizing your desk, books, or bedroom • Playing card games • Playing office or organizing a project • Setting up play space or work areas	**BUSINESS** • Accounting • Business Computer Apps. • Business Law • Business Presentations • Career Planning • Cooperative Work Experience • Desktop Publishing • Fashion Apparel and Accessories • Fashion Marketing • Financial Planning • Introduction to Business • Marketing and Advertising • Sports Management and Marketing • Wall Street I and II **MATH** • Algebra • Calculus • Computer Science • Computers: Visual Basic • Geometry • Programming for the Web • Statistics • Trigonometry	• Academic Quiz Bowl • DECA, FBLA • Math Team

Conventional, or the Organizers, are people who like to work with data, have clerical or numerical ability, carry out tasks in detail, or follow through on others' instructions.

Internship Options	2-Year College Majors	4-Year College Majors
• Accounting office • Camp office • Data processing/ computer firm • Doctor's office—medical records • Law office • Library	• Computer Information Systems • Food Service Administration • Medical Records • Office Technologies • Administrative Assistant • Executive • Informational Processing • Legal • Paralegal Studies	• Accounting • Accounting Technology • Administrative Office Technology • Data Processing • Financial Services • Information Services and Support • Information Systems • Legal Assisting/Pre-Law Studies • Paralegal Studies • Secretarial Technology • Spanish & Legal Assisting • Transportation Management Technology
Sample of Professions		
• Accountant • Budget Analyst • Building or Safety Inspector	• Business Teacher • Insurance Claims/ Collections • Librarian	• Mortgage Expeditor • Paralegal • Real Estate Title Clerk

PART VI

Ready, Set, Play

14

What's Your Career DNA?

To assist you in discovering your Career DNA interest code, you can use one of the following quick assessments designed for young children, teens or adults. We have also supplied a play sheet area in the next section to help you keep track of your results.

Remember, a complete Career DNA assessment, which would include evaluations for the other key elements, should be done with a professional career consultant.

Quick Assessment One—Young Children

Observing the toys and games children love to play can lead to successful education and career choices later. Here is a quick assessment that will pinpoint a child's career strength using an interest type. Check off all the toys or games your child likes the <u>most</u> in each group. The highest total is your child's dominant interest. The second and third highest are secondary influences.

GAMES, TOYS, AND ACTIVITIES OF INTEREST FOR YOUNG CHILDREN

Group R **REALISTIC**	**Group I** **INVESTIGATIVE**	**Group A** **ARTISTIC**
☐ Logs or building blocks ☐ Radio controlled toys ☐ Sports ☐ Toy tool and building sets ☐ Toy trucks or action figures	☐ Archaeology/ dinosaur kit ☐ Bug collecting or Fossil making kit ☐ Scavenger hunts ☐ Telescope or microscope ☐ Toy doctor or chemistry sets	☐ Arts and crafts ☐ Modeling clay ☐ Painting, coloring, drawing ☐ Play acting ☐ Sewing or ceramics
TOTAL _____	TOTAL _____	TOTAL _____
Group S **SOCIAL**	**Group E** **ENTERPRISING**	**Group C** **CONVENTIONAL**
☐ Community youth groups ☐ Dolls or stuffed animals ☐ Group or team games ☐ Playing nurse or doctor ☐ Playing school	☐ Piggy bank savings ☐ Playing board games such as chess, checkers or Monopoly™ ☐ Playing grocery store or bank ☐ Setting up & running a carwash or lemonade stand ☐ Strategy and simulation games	☐ Collecting baseball cards ☐ Collecting stamps or coins ☐ Organizing books and papers ☐ Organizing room or closet ☐ Playing office and organizing desk
TOTAL _____	TOTAL _____	TOTAL _____

(Refer back to the Career DNA Synopsis in Part V for interest details)

Quick Assessment Two—Teens

Teenagers have different activities and interests that can more clearly define their higher education and career choices. Have teenagers evaluate the conversation choices below and choose the top three groups they would prefer at a peer teen party. This will reveal the authentic interests element of their personal Career DNA.

CONVERSATION CHOICES AT A PARTY FOR TEENS

Group R	Group I	Group A
REALISTIC	**INVESTIGATIVE**	**ARTISTIC**
People are talking about:	**People are talking about:**	**People are talking about:**
☐ cooking a meal ☐ going hiking ☐ operating a computer ☐ playing sports ☐ playing video games ☐ repairing a car	☐ finding lost treasure ☐ playing detective ☐ the last book they read ☐ using a chemistry set ☐ using a microscope	☐ acting in a play ☐ drawing pictures ☐ going to an art museum or craft show ☐ playing an instrument
TOTAL _____	**TOTAL** _____	**TOTAL** _____

Group S	Group E	Group C
SOCIAL	**ENTERPRISING**	**CONVENTIONAL**
People are talking about:	**People are talking about:**	**People are talking about:**
☐ going out with their friends ☐ going to the mall ☐ helping other people ☐ reading books to children ☐ what is happening at school	☐ following the stock market ☐ playing board games ☐ raising money ☐ setting up a car wash ☐ starting a business	☐ discussing a favorite collection of articles ☐ organizing a project ☐ setting up a work or play space ☐ their baseball card collection
TOTAL _____	**TOTAL** _____	**TOTAL** _____

(Refer back to the Career DNA Synopsis in Part V for interest details)

Quick Assessment Three—Adults

Adults can easily assess and determine their interest code by considering their business and social activities. Assume you are going to a networking event by yourself. When you arrive, you see there are tables with six groups of people who each have similar interests or traits. Choose the top three groups of people you would feel most comfortable joining. Match the group letter of your first, second, and third interest choices to solve your career success puzzle.

INTEREST GROUP CHOICES AT NETWORKING EVENT FOR ADULTS[3]

Group R	Group I	Group A
REALISTIC	**INVESTIGATIVE**	**ARTISTIC**
Doers	*Thinkers*	*Creators*
People who are athletic or have mechanical ability, prefer to work with objects, machines, tools, plants, or animals, or to be outdoors.	People who like to observe, learn, investigate, analyze, evaluate, or solve problems.	People who have artistic, innovative, or intuitional abilities and like to work in unstructured situations using their imagination and creativity.
TOTAL _____	TOTAL _____	TOTAL _____
Group S	Group E	Group C
SOCIAL	**ENTERPRISING**	**CONVENTIONAL**
Helpers	*Persuaders*	*Organizers*
People who like to work with other people to enlighten, inform, help, train, or cure them, or are skilled with words.	People who like to work with people, influencing, persuading, performing, leading, or managing for organizational goals or economic gain.	People who like to work with data, have clerical or numerical ability, carry out tasks in detail, or follow through on others' instructions.
TOTAL _____	TOTAL _____	TOTAL _____

(Refer back to the Career DNA Synopsis in Part V for interest details)

Games2Careers Play Sheet

*(Journal your assessment results,
interests, ideas, and questions)*

_____

_____

_____

_____

_____

_____

_____

_____

_____

_____

_____

_____

About the Authors

Susan H. Gubing

Named a Professional Who Makes an Impact on Long Island's Economy by *Newsday*, Susan H. Gubing is a leader in industry and education consulting. As principal of her consulting firm, CareerSmarts, Susan has been instrumental in guiding scores of young adults to realize their career goals. For over forty years, she has educated and assisted her students through the career process using the application of Holland Codes.

Susan has been an instructor, career counselor, and workforce development coordinator for the State of New York College at Oswego and has worked extensively for the Smithtown Central School District in New York. Some of her clients include the State of New York Education Department, Long Island Works Coalition, Long Island Mentoring, BOCES, and several colleges.

Susan Gubing is available for keynote speaking. You may contact her by e-mail at Sue@careersmarts.com or by phone at 631.979.6452. For more information about CareerSmarts, please visit her site at www.careersmarts.com.

Karen McKenna

Karen McKenna is a corporate training specialist and career adviser who worked for the Estée Lauder Companies, Drake Beam Morin (DBM), the Council for Adult and Experiential Learning (CAEL), JPMorgan Chase Career Services, and Winthrop University Hospital. She has designed and delivered training programs on technical skills, interpersonal communication skills, customer service excellence, and management development.

Karen is passionate about helping people to achieve career success. She served as a mentor through Big Brothers Big Sisters of Long Island from 1997 through 2004 and was honored as Big Sister of the Year 2000 for New York State. As a seasoned professional and volunteer, Karen has delivered presentations to a variety of audiences by sharing her experiences as a mentor and raising awareness for Big Brothers Big Sisters programs

Currently, Karen is the senior program manager of Career Paths at Tuesday's Children, a nonprofit family service organization. She provides career guidance for those directly affected by the terror attacks on September 11, 2001. Karen resides in East Setauket, New York, with her husband, Richard Bergius.

Dear Reader,

We sincerely hope you have enjoyed Games2Careers. *In case you are wondering, here are our Career DNA interest codes:*

Susan H. Gubing

ESC—Enterprising, Social, and Conventional

Karen McKenna

SAE—Social, Artistic, and Enterprising

We have two interests in common: enterprising and social. Although the strength of these interests varies for each of us, the combination highlights our mutual interest in working with people. We have no doubt that the similarities led each of us, as individuals, to become career counselors.

Our shared interests also brought us together in the writing of this book, an endeavor that was a smooth and enjoyable experience. As it turned out, it was our diversity—one being artistic and the other conventional—that brought balance to the technical and creative aspects necessary in publishing a book.

Thank you for playing the career success game with us.

Best wishes,
Susan and Karen

To learn more about Games*2*Careers, please visit www.games2careers.com.

You will find valuable self-assessment tools and resources to assist in current and future educational and career planning.

Printed in the United States
146468LV00001B/1/A